CHARLIE LE MINDU

ROADS Publishing
19–22 Dame Street
Dublin 2
Ireland

www.roads.co

First published 2015

1

Charlie Le Mindu
Haute Coiffure
Images copyright © the copyright holders,p.255
Design by Conor & David

Printed in Italy by Graphicom s.r.l

Cover image:
© Inès Dieleman

978-1-909399-64-8

CHARLIE LE MINDU

HAUTE COIFFURE

ROADS

PUBLISHING

This book is very special for me, because it gathers together so much of my work, and it reminds me of all the things that have inspired my collections.

I have always been influenced by film-makers like John Waters and Pedro Almodóvar. I love their casting the most. They celebrate individuality, and they don't shy away from ugly, crazy characters.

But I'm also very inspired by women. My work has continuously strived to create a new kind of woman, a girl with her own character and attitude – a fearless person with so much intensity and power that she both attracts and scares others.

The spirit of punk is the lifeblood of my work; without it my art wouldn't be so raw. I don't want to listen to politics, and I never open fashion magazines. I don't want those kind of influences; I prefer to go out, to dance and to listen to people's stories. That is what really inspires me. Punk and electronica helped me become the way I am, but I describe myself as a gypsy because I'm not attached to any world: I prefer creating my own one.

My work is constantly evolving, and recently my passion has shifted more towards performance and exhibitions. I love performance because it is then that my work comes alive. When you work with hair it's so satisfying to see lots of movement. I've been exhibiting internationally since 2009, and that holds a different appeal. It shows my work in a completely new light, and I love to see how people respond to it in this kind of environment.

Will I ever do a catwalk again? Time will tell. But now is the perfect time to celebrate all of my catwalk work in this book, alongside my favourite collaborations – with my friends, and with amazing photographers like Nick Knight, Rankin, Ellen von Unwerth and Tim Walker.

In many ways, *Haute Coiffure* mirrors my career. Creating it has been like creating a show, which is all about movement and bringing the pieces to life; the finished book is like an exhibition piece, to be revisited and enjoyed forever. This book brings me a lot of happiness. It documents my life so far, and all of my work, and it reminds me of my best friends. In the end, they are why my work is so colourful.

—Charlie Le Mindu

…'s said that real madmen don't realise they're crazy, while self-professed ones are perfectly sane. 'I'm not insane,' Charlie Le Mindu has insisted to me, setting off all the alarm bells that should be ringing around an artistic mind of his calibre. Call him mad or simply eccentric, the key to his unique creativity is the fact that he is oblivious to his own shock value. From his haute coiffure to haute couture, the word 'extreme' is inescapably associated with Charlie. But whether he's sent naked women down his runway, dressed superstars in fantastical wigs, or taken radical measures with his own body, Charlie's art has always been born out of emotional impulse rather than a need to impress. I think it's all he knows.

'He's a unique character,' Nicola Formichetti tells me. Lady Gaga's former creative director, Formichetti commissioned the larger-than-life hair costumes Charlie made for the singer, and has worked with him ever since. 'Charlie is multi-talented. He's a bit of a hairdresser, a bit of a designer, a bit of an outsider – and an insider. When we collaborate it's always interesting. He can go so many ways.' Speak to Peaches, one of Charlie's oldest friends and collaborators, and she'll back that up. 'Charlie has a way of sweeping you up into his world. When we "work" we are constantly laughing and telling stories, and by the end of it I am completely transformed without even realising that he has started.'

When I met Charlie he was already a superstar on the East London club scene. He had arrived from Berlin on New Year's Day 2008, catching the tail end of the club kid movement that washed over the city in the mid '00s. Tired of techno, he was infatuated with pop and eager to break the fashion world with which he'd just been acquainted. In many ways, the audacity of a hairdresser deciding to be a designer and putting on a fashion show captured the architect-of-your-own-fortune spirit of the arts scene in Recession London, and by the time his fully naked runway models from the *Detox Retox Botox* collection ended up in newspapers worldwide in the autumn of 2010, I knew a star was born.

For all his wig-making skills and talent as a colourist, Charlie's success lies in his irreverent social commentary as an artist. He has based his shows on consumerism, celebrity culture, veganism, and whatever else fashion's pseudo-intellectual snobs scoffed at, praising it and rolling his eyes at it all at once. 'He is a rebel and a revolutionary,' Anna Trevelyan says. A close friend of Charlie's, she has styled many of his London Fashion Week shows. 'He is open-minded, never judgemental, and always giggling about something naughty and causing trouble. Not many people actually embody the real meaning of punk.'

Back in France, it was punk that first resonated with a teenage Charlie in the late '90s. Born in Bergerac in 1986, he was raised in the slow-life wine country of Castelnau-de-Médoc, the working-class son of a 'rugby man' construction worker and an eccentric cleaning lady with a penchant for Nina Hagen. Young Charlie would delight in his mother's pleather all-in-ones ('she looked like a prostitute'), take note when she declared how much

better Michael Jackson looked post-cosmetic surgery, and make his parents watch as he choreographed performances with the little brother he had dressed up in full *Priscilla, Queen of the Desert* gear. His first cassette tape was – but of course – Cher's *Believe*.

For a fat, gay kid, life outside of the home was less fabulous. The severe bullying he experienced as a young teenager at school accelerated his dream of becoming a hairdresser, and at fourteen, Charlie as good as said goodbye to school to start his apprenticeship, glamming up provincial French ladies and obsessing over old-school hairdressing methods. 'When everyone was doing asymmetrical haircuts, all I wanted to do was put rollers on grandmothers,' he recalls. An intense young man, Charlie got fired from five salons, something that only added to his street cred in the arty punk circles he'd begun frequenting in Bordeaux, where he was now living with his first boyfriend.

'Charlie was insane because he was experimenting with everything. He was going in every direction; super wild,' the artist Coralie Ruiz, Charlie's close friend since their teenage years, reminisces. 'He was determined to be the best, and wanted to go to Hollywood to be hairdresser to the stars!' It was, however, the debauched club scene of Berlin that became the setting for Charlie's first adventure. With an admitted sexual drive above average ('I have a huge problem with sex. I like it too much'), he'd had his first sexual encounter at the age of nine and spent his teenage years exploring his desires.

A haven for extreme personalities, Berlin's nightlife became the natural culmination of a rocky adolescence. Eighteen years old and defying his provincial inhibitions to the max, Charlie met his spirit animals in the shape of the club scene's sensational drag queens – something he'd never seen before – and began creating spectacular wigs for them. And like *Moulin Rouge!* but gayer and with techno, the country boy became a poet of the night, cutting people's hair in clubs as part of theatrical installations, from manscaping the bears at Festsaal Kreuzberg and Berghain, to cutting club kids' hair on stage at Barbie Deinhoff's, dressed as a giant rabbit while a drag queen, he fondly recalls, 'put carrots up my ass'.

It was at such a club night – *Hair Doctor* at Rio – that Charlie met Peaches. 'He had a lot of attitude and Berlin was not big enough for him,' the singer recalls. 'I remember when he told me he was going to move to London and start making fashion. I had nothing but complete confidence in him.' Longing to replace his dark nightlife existence in Berlin with something new and happier, Charlie had been advised by Liz Bisoux and Nova Dando – East London royalty – to come to the city's fashion week, ruled at the time by a core of young irreverent designers such as Gareth Pugh and Giles Deacon. Peaches introduced him to the B-52s, and soon enough, Charlie was touring England as the band's hairdresser, planning his big move to London.

I first heard about Charlie as the wig-maker to Lady Gaga. He arrived in London just a year before she reached the height of

her career with 'Bad Romance' in 2009, a video that featured a lip-shaped wig Charlie created for her. Gaga had branded her style somewhat through anti-establishment designers, of whom there were plenty in London, but in a fashion industry that demands business savvy and discipline, those young designers rarely led the alternative lives associated with their work. Charlie, of course, was the exception. Completely un-British, he said and did the most preposterous things and got away with it all in the name of his brand of eccentricity. 'It was a very avant-garde moment in time, very surreal,' Nicola Formichetti recalls. 'Charlie's medium was hair so it really fitted with what we wanted to do at that time.'

It was just Charlie being Charlie, but it made real the impulsive and fiercely creative culture reflected in the image of Lady Gaga. 'Charlie has no limits, and this is very important to understand in terms of his career,' Coralie Ruiz tells me. 'At the same time, he is a very subtle, authentic person, and I find this fascinating. He is himself in any situation, in front of any type of person: a politician, an old man, a punk, or his mum. He is also a very tolerant human being,' she notes. Anna Trevelyan explains, 'He creates his work without boundaries or fear, and it comes truly from an original and personal place. I can see how every single thing he creates connects to him personally and his experiences and ideas.'

In my eyes, the success Charlie experienced during his first years in London was a result of his believability: you knew his life off the runway was as mad as the things he sent down it. Case in point, Peaches tells me about her first experience at Charlie's always-mobile hair salon. 'During a DJ gig I had in London, he hid under the DJ booth before I started playing and the plan was that in the middle of the set, I would spin a long track and duck under while he dyed my hair. Then forty-five minutes later, I would duck under again and he would wash and style it. He was crouched down there with his blow-dryer and his mixing bowl, ready for action. We couldn't stop laughing.'

Soon, Charlie had become a London fashion phenomenon. Next to his high-profile gigs – he was, for instance, the first hairdresser to give Florence Welch of Florence + the Machine her signature red dye job – his seasonal fashion shows were getting bigger and more grotesque, ranging from super pop to super trash but always keeping a confident female character in the spotlight. His *Berlin Syndrome* collection for autumn/winter 2011 opened with a naked girl covered in fake blood wearing a headpiece featuring the word 'violence'. Charlie took his bow in a bloody apron, a butcher's knife in hand. 'I didn't want to shock people, I wanted to convey a feeling,' he says, years after. 'Shocking people is stupid. What's the point of shocking someone just for a reaction?'

London, local Shoreditch superstar Jamie Bull. While exploring religious themes in the collections *Burka Curfew* (spring/summer 2012) and *Kosher Dreams* (spring/summer 2013), Charlie returned to his own religious roots, his youth's obsession with cosmetically enhanced pop stars and a fascination with radically changing his own appearance. Deciding that his already rather widespread collection of tattoos wasn't quite enough, after an epic weight loss Charlie had his torso surgically enhanced through extensive liposculpture.

While he took the plastic surgery in his typical *laissez-faire* stride, his transformation marked a new chapter in the life and work of Charlie Le Mindu. It seemed he became chicer – a little more Parisian, if you will – and with it, so did his fashion. *Metal Queen* for spring/summer 2013 was Charlie's first show on the hallowed haute couture schedule in Paris, and his ultimate foray into the *savoir-vivre* of fashion. The fat, gay kid from Castelnau-de-Médoc, who became a punk hairdresser and raved in Berlin, was suddenly showing 1980s-style salon shows of painstakingly handcrafted garments in Paris, and taking his bow in luxe body-con tops that showed off his artificial abs. He even married – Thomas Petherick, a British set designer, and stayed married for two years. For Charlie, I think it was the most punk stage of his life.

'People might think he's a bit of a crazy person, but his attention to detail is impeccable,' Nicola Formichetti tells me. 'Sometimes when you see the work of an avant-garde designer, it looks great from afar but it's a mess up close. As a hairdresser you have to be really precise in every millimetre of your creation, and that's what sets him apart and what I love about him.' For Charlie, work never seemed like something he pushed himself to do, but something he couldn't resist. The crazier his creations get, the more hours he puts into them. Call it an addiction or a *condition*, his compulsion to create things, share them with people, and feel their emotional reaction is what makes him the brilliant madman I've always thought he was.

'I think it's very chic. Chic is a mentality,' Charlie will say about his work. And while it may have little in common with the minimalist beige cashmere coats that usually receive that fashion stamp of *chic*, there's something to be said for the elegance portrayed through Charlie's work. Because it is always about personality and emotion, an integrity shines through those out-of-this-world creations that ultimately could only be described as chic. Hell, the fact that he can't really sell any of it is pretty chic in itself. 'I'm not a fashion person,' he'll say with perfect French dismissal. 'I don't want to sell people tops and trousers, I want to sell feelings.'

— Anders Christian Madsen

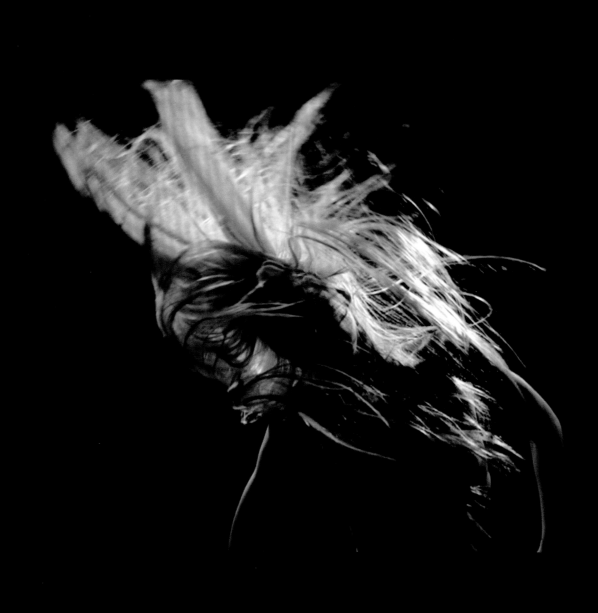

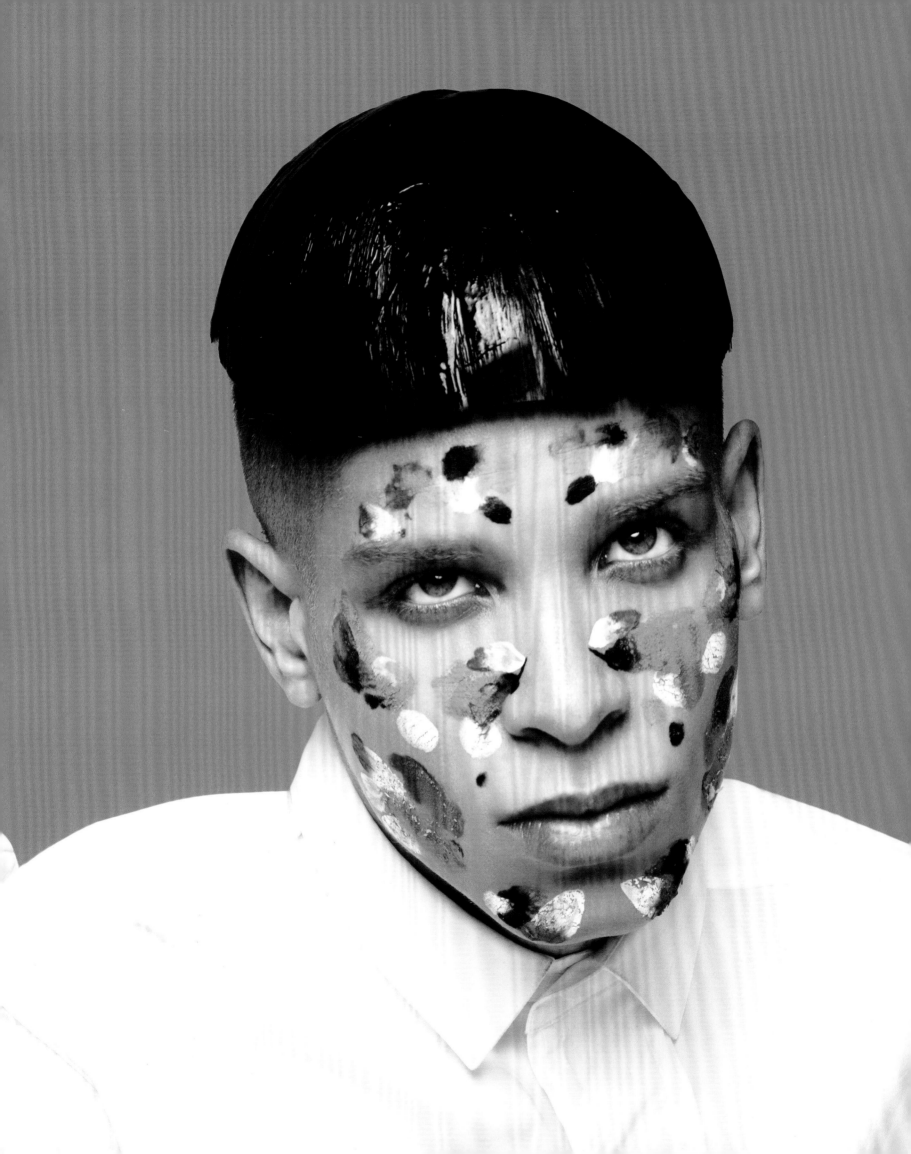

Charlie has a way of sweeping you up into his world. When we 'work' we are constantly laughing and telling stories, and by the end of it I am completely transformed without even realising that he has started.
　—Peaches

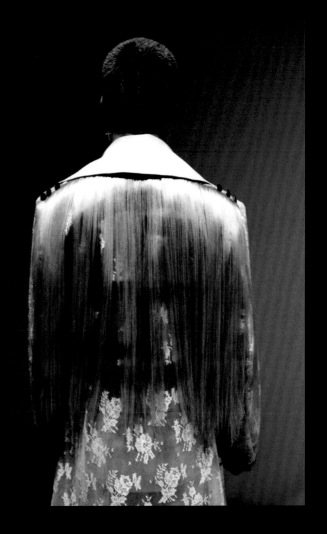

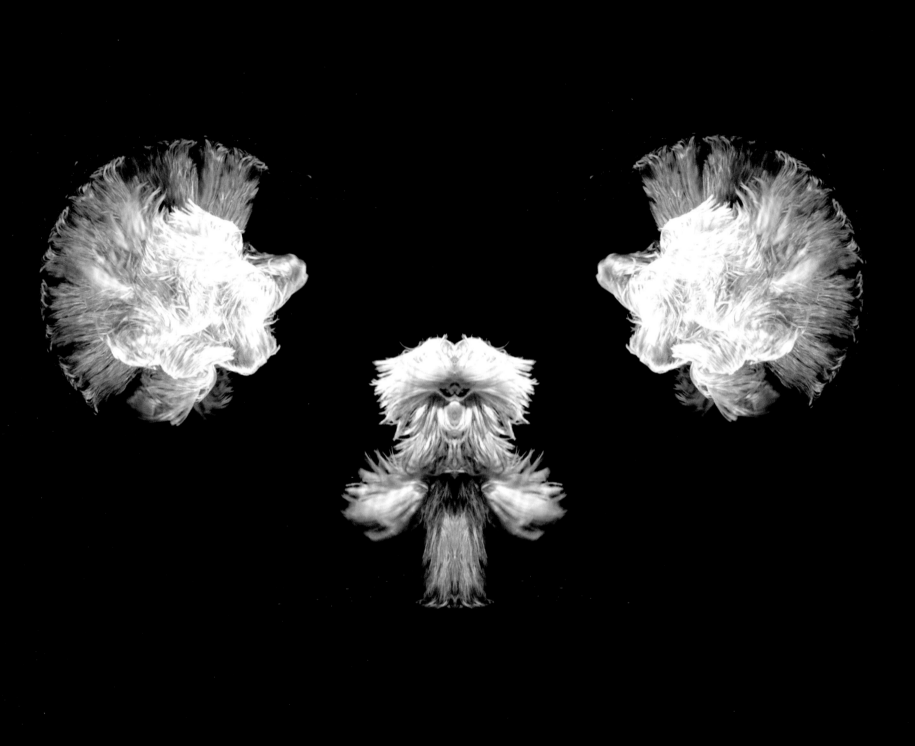

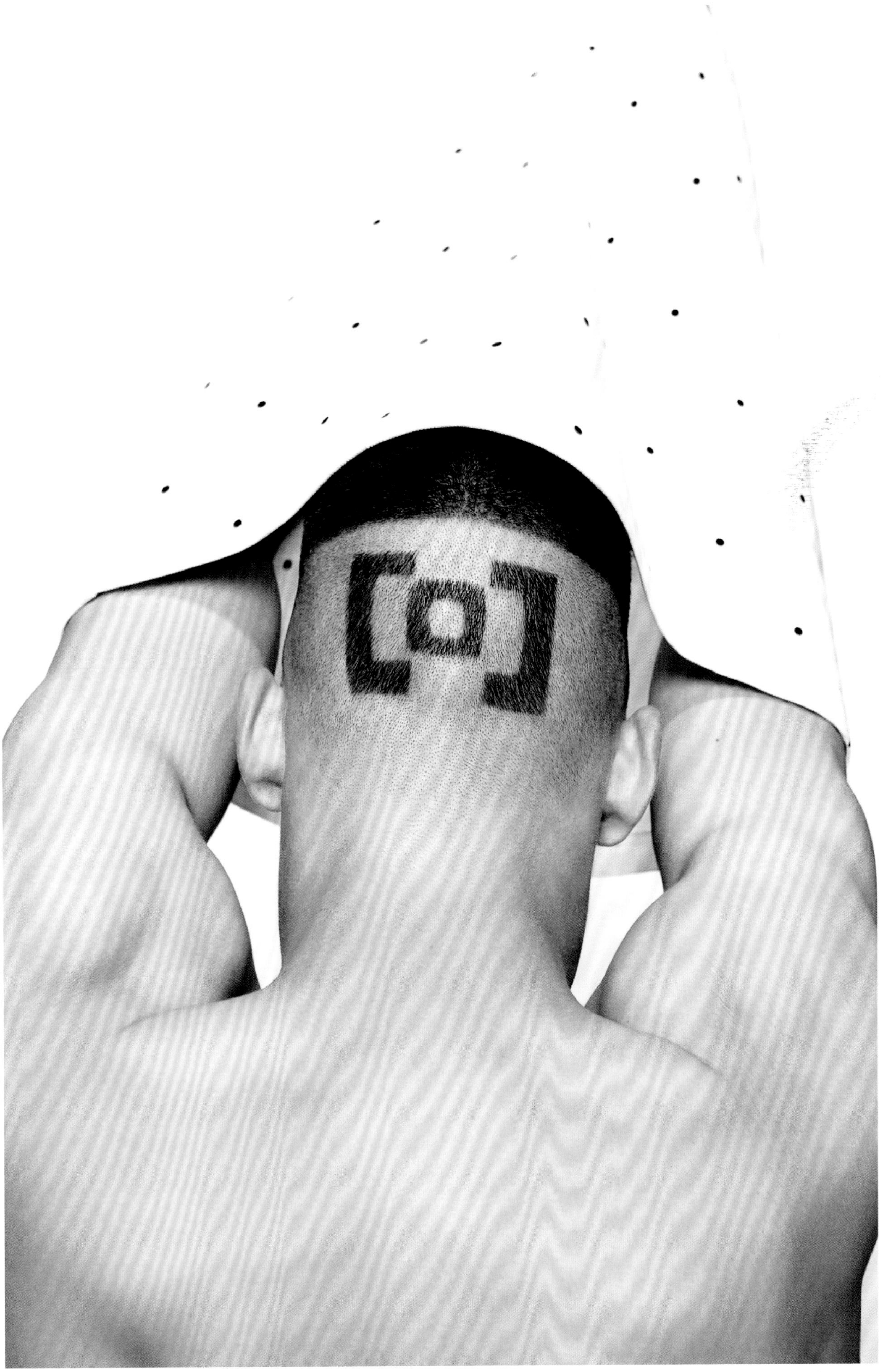

Charlie is a brilliant, funny gentleman with boundless creativity and a truly innovative artistic sensibility. He has so much talent; it's fascinating to watch him create pieces from his obsessions. I enjoy every time I see Charlie, but walking in his S/S12 Paris show as Cleopatra was amazing. He really is a master of hair.
—Rossy De Palma

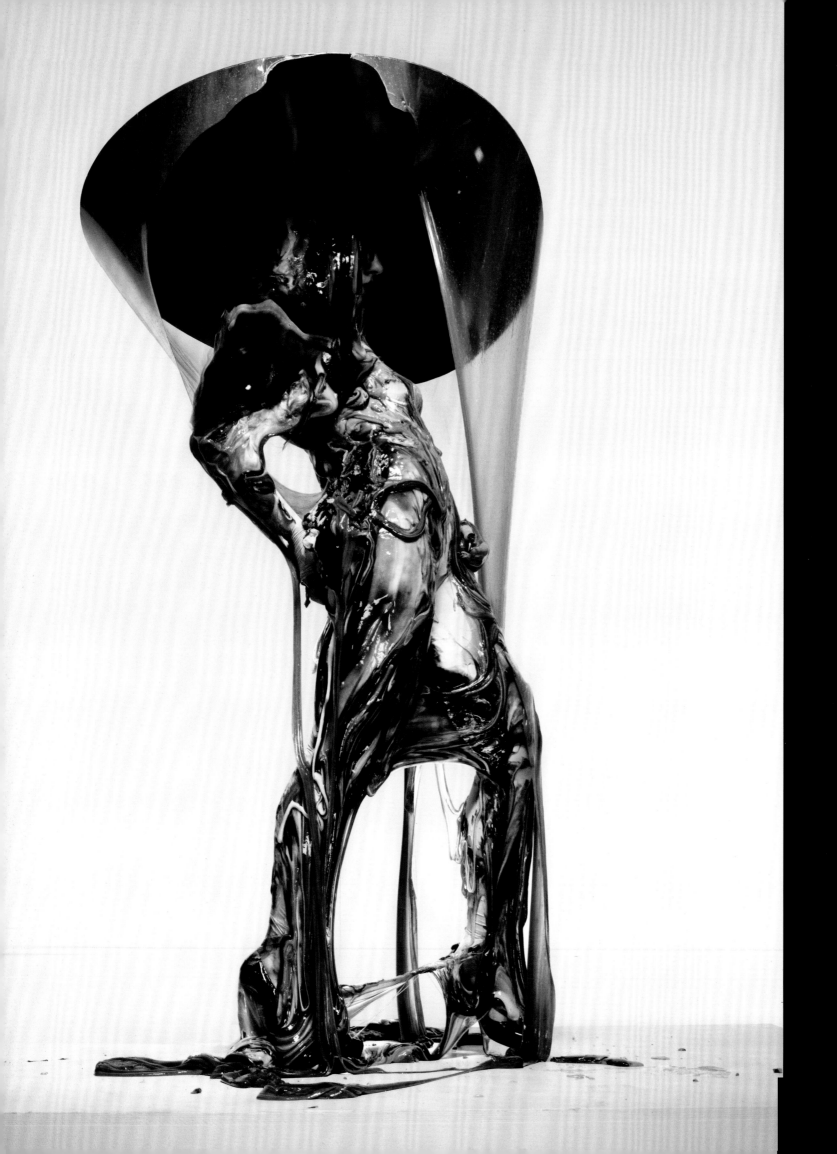

Le Mindu is a unique character. He's a bit of a hairdresser, a bit of a designer, a bit of an outsider — *and* an insider. People might think he's a bit of a crazy person, but his attention to detail is impeccable — that's what sets him apart.
   —Nicola Formichetti

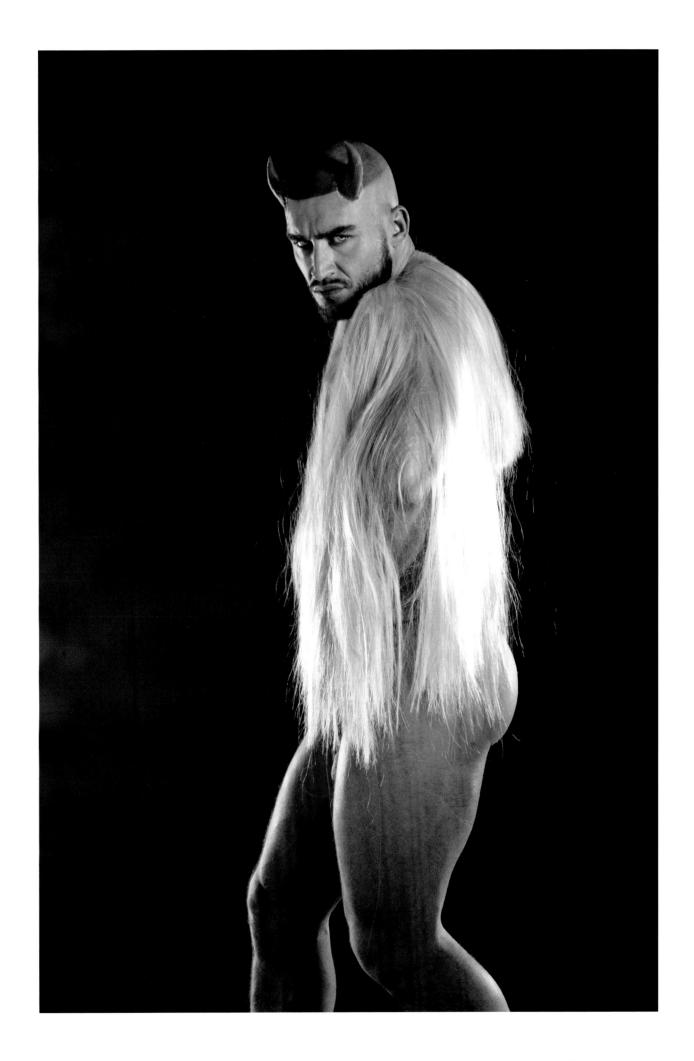

Charlie and I have worked together a number of times, and he's an extremely generous collaborator. For my *Incubus* movie project I had a very clear vision of the evil goat costumes that I wanted. I presented Charlie with my drawings and he executed them exactly the way I wanted them, and surprisingly quickly. I was so impressed, it was almost magical … I felt like a spoiled child!

Charlie works as a designer each season, of course, and follows the rhythm of the fashion calendar, but his work is more about style than trends. He creates his own worlds, and the unifying thread is his medium: hair. What a fabulous artistic concept. I guess he doesn't follow the rules that much.

—François Sagat

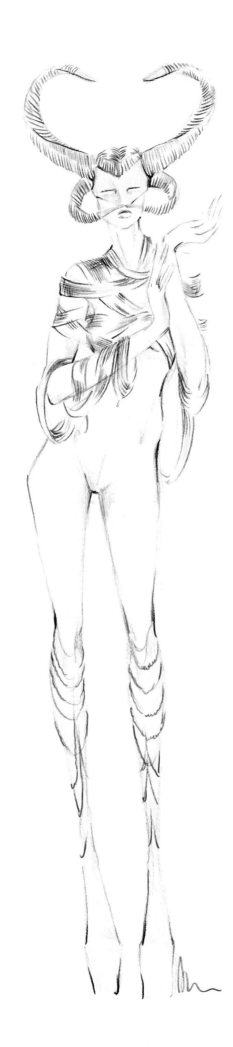

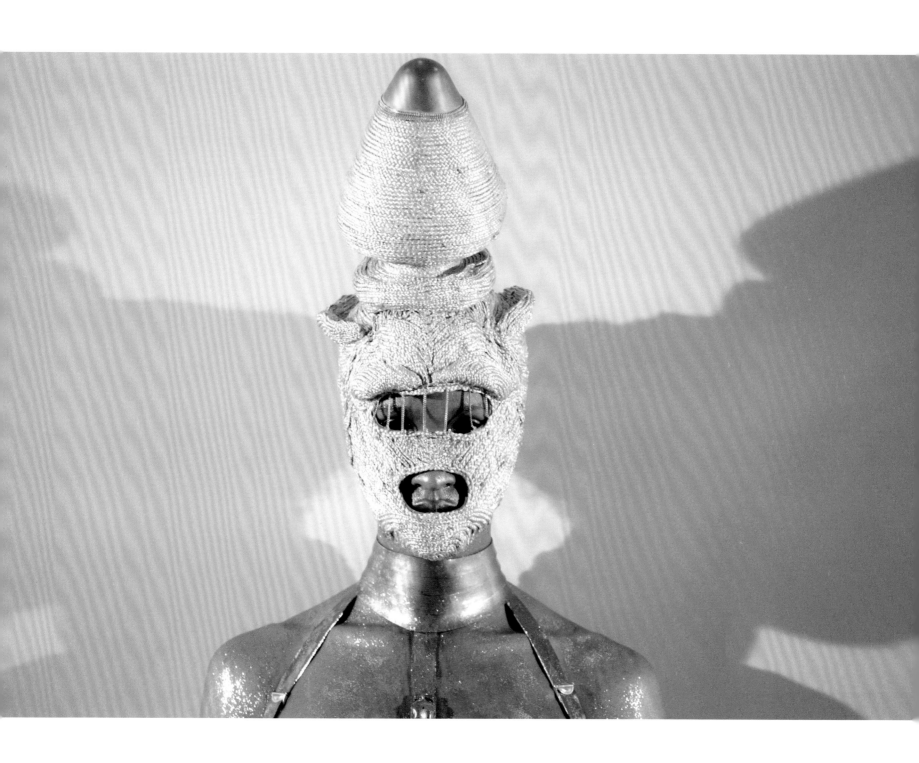

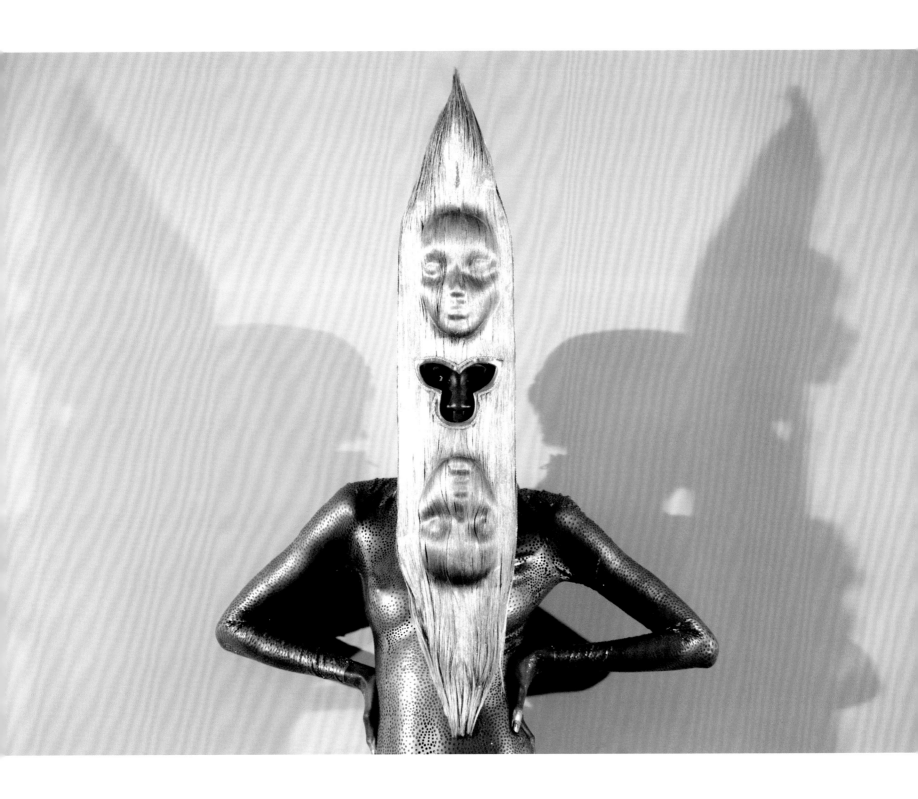

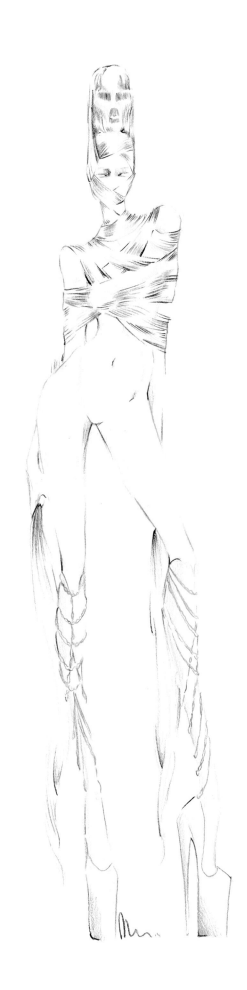

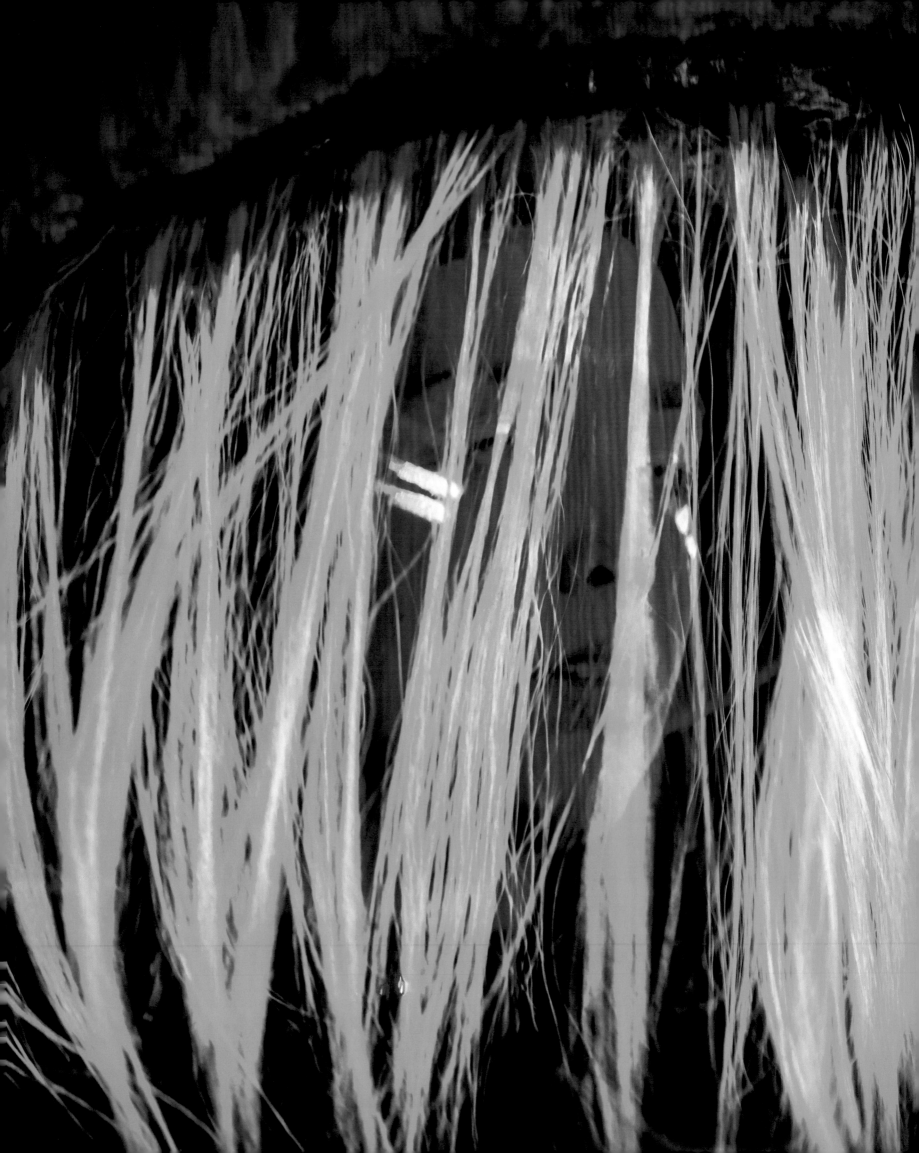

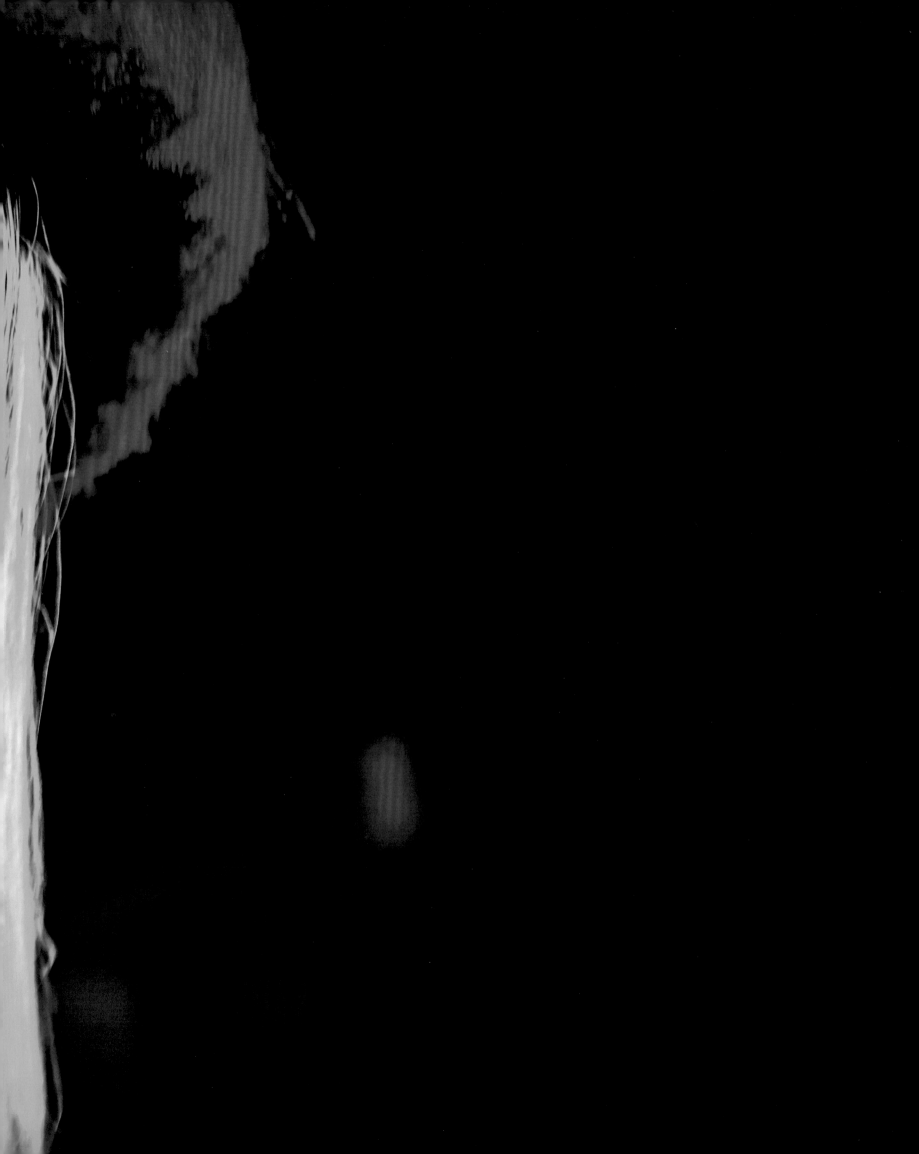

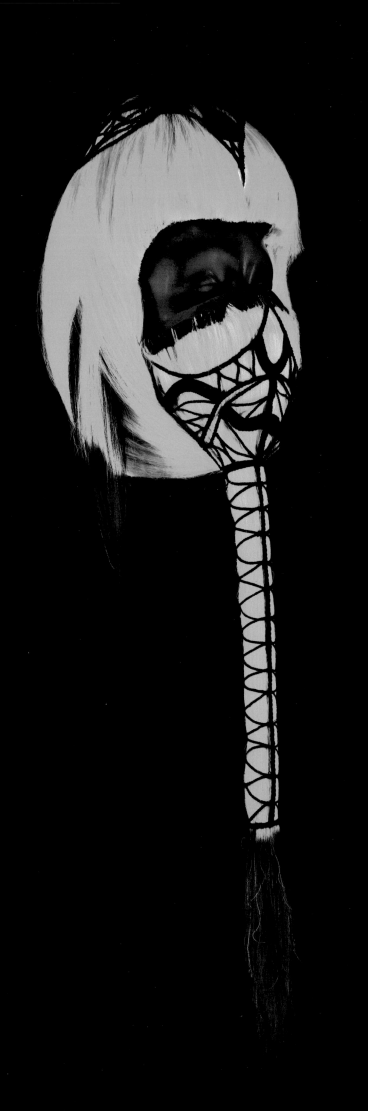

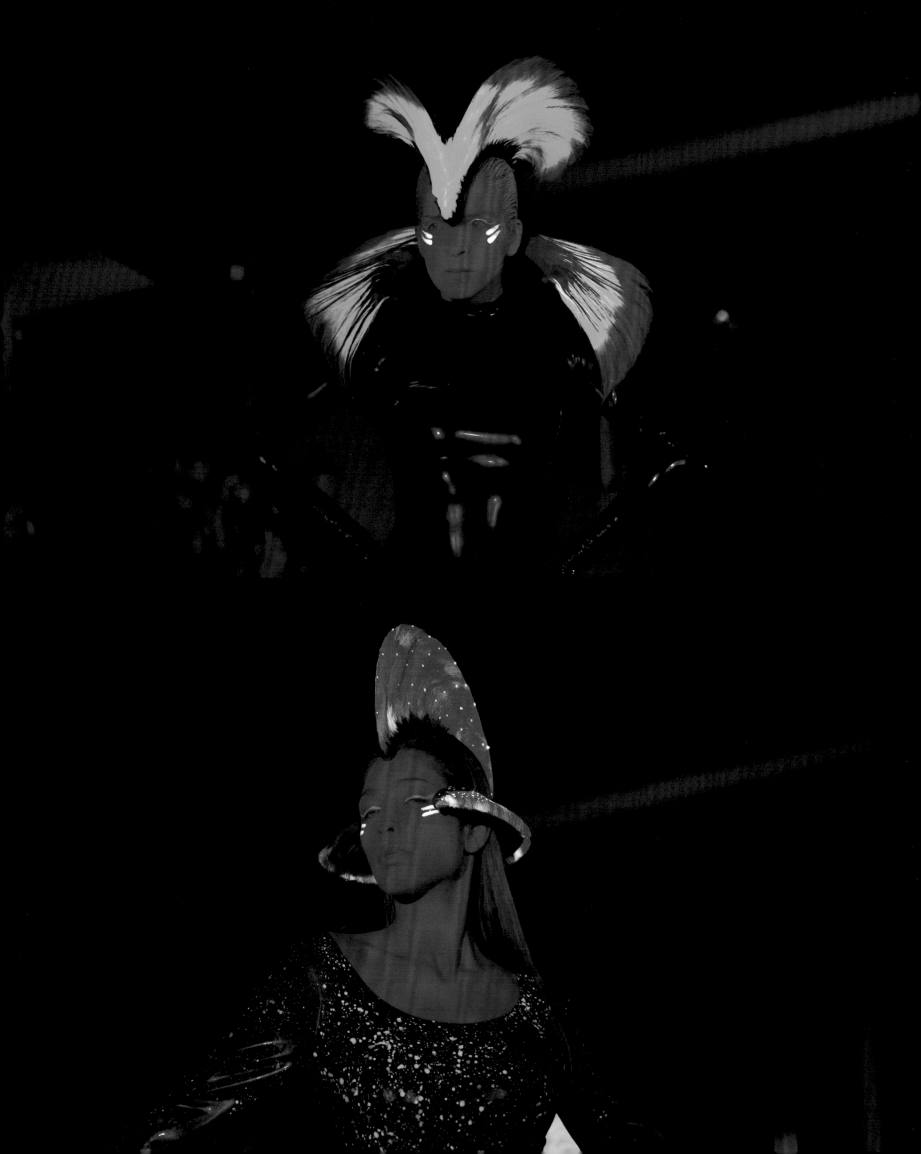

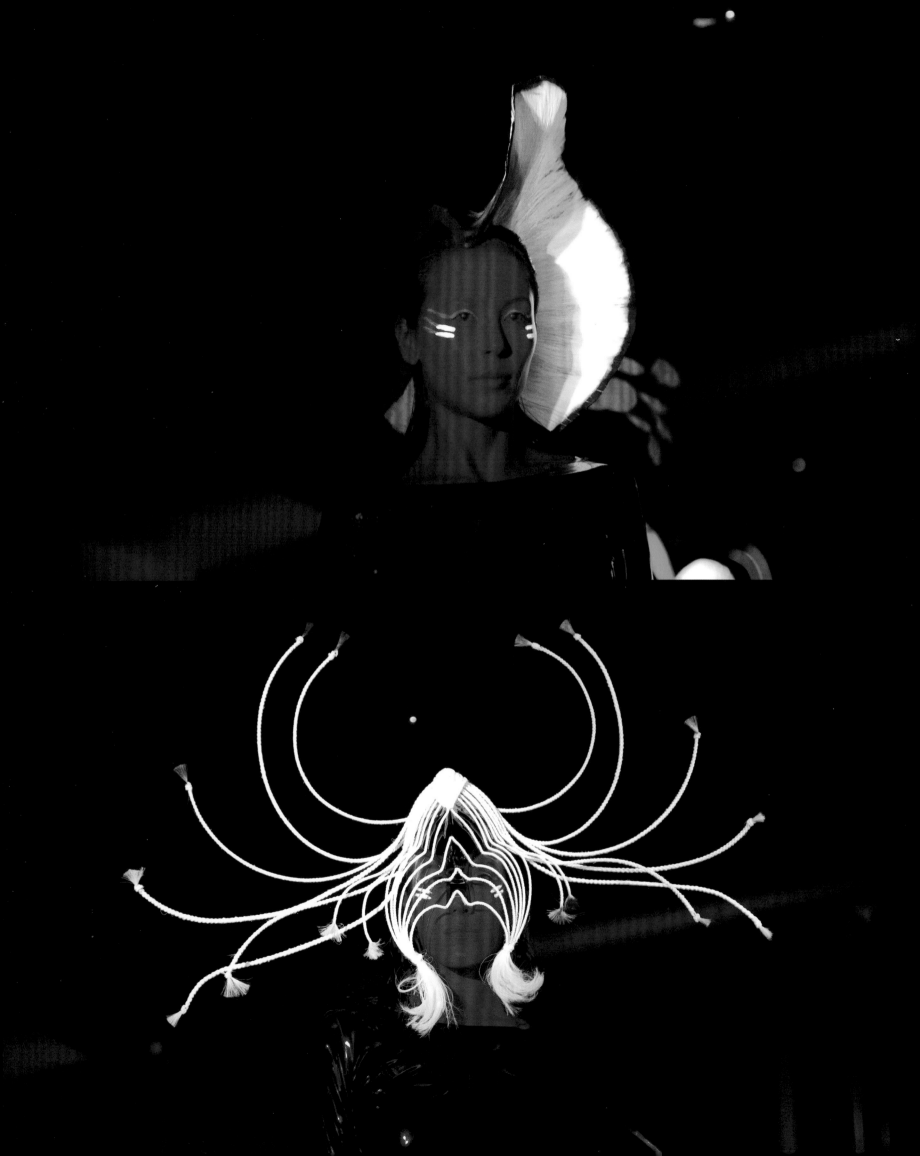

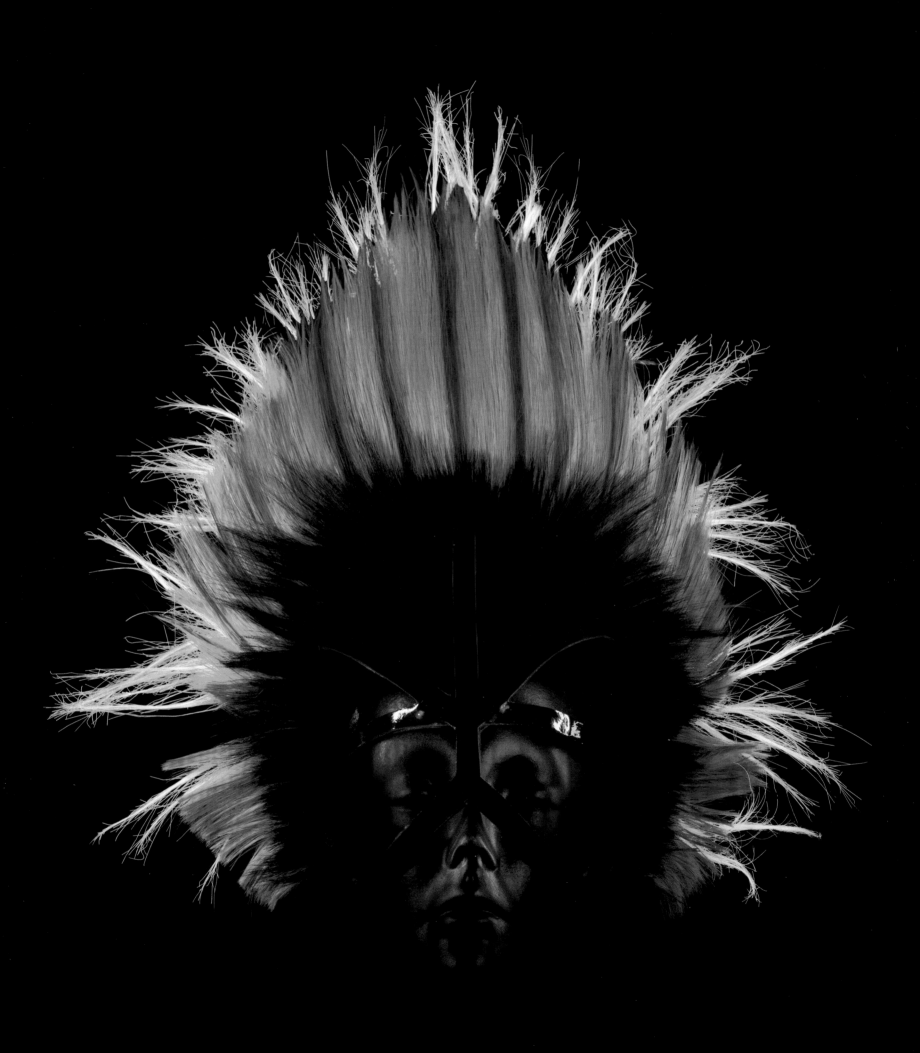

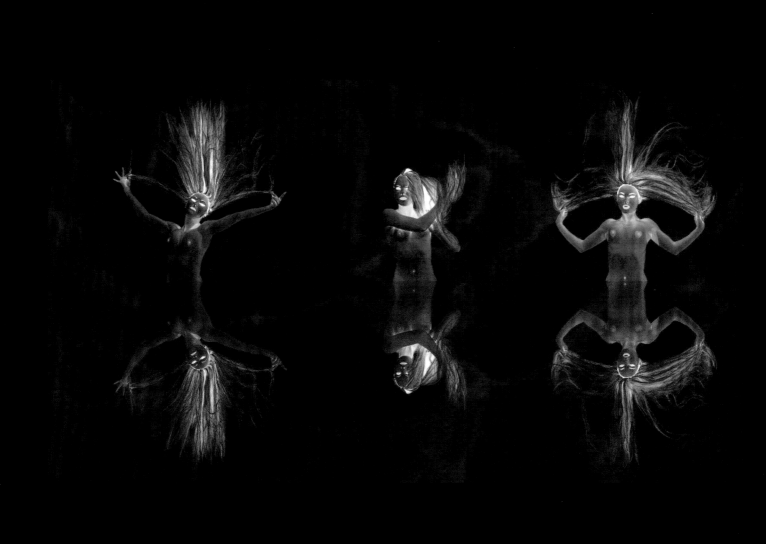

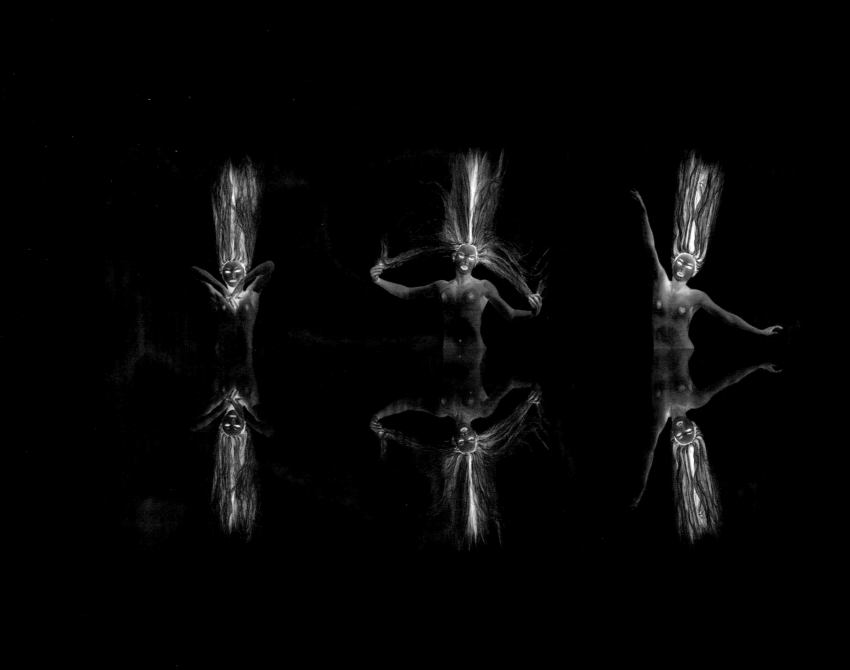

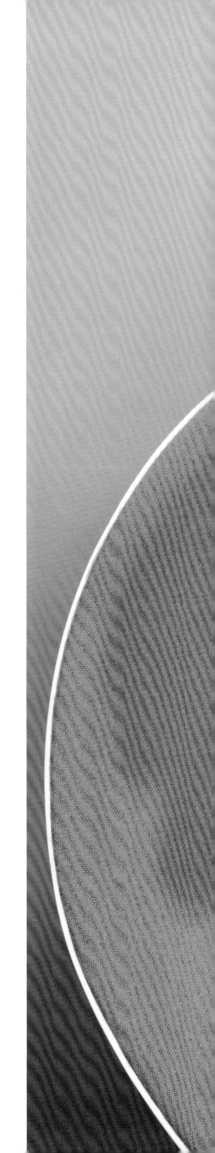

Charlie looks so sweet and shy, but he definitely has a naughty twin. He is a real artist; not only does he know how to do great hair for fashion stories, but he also creates amazing, inspiring pieces with hair that remind me of scenes from twentieth-century movies and cabarets. It's amazing to work with him backstage at his shows, and to watch him create on the spot. Recently, I had a great time working with him on the Life Ball poster with Conchita Wurst. Oh, and I love it when he shows me his tattoos!
—Ellen von Unwerth

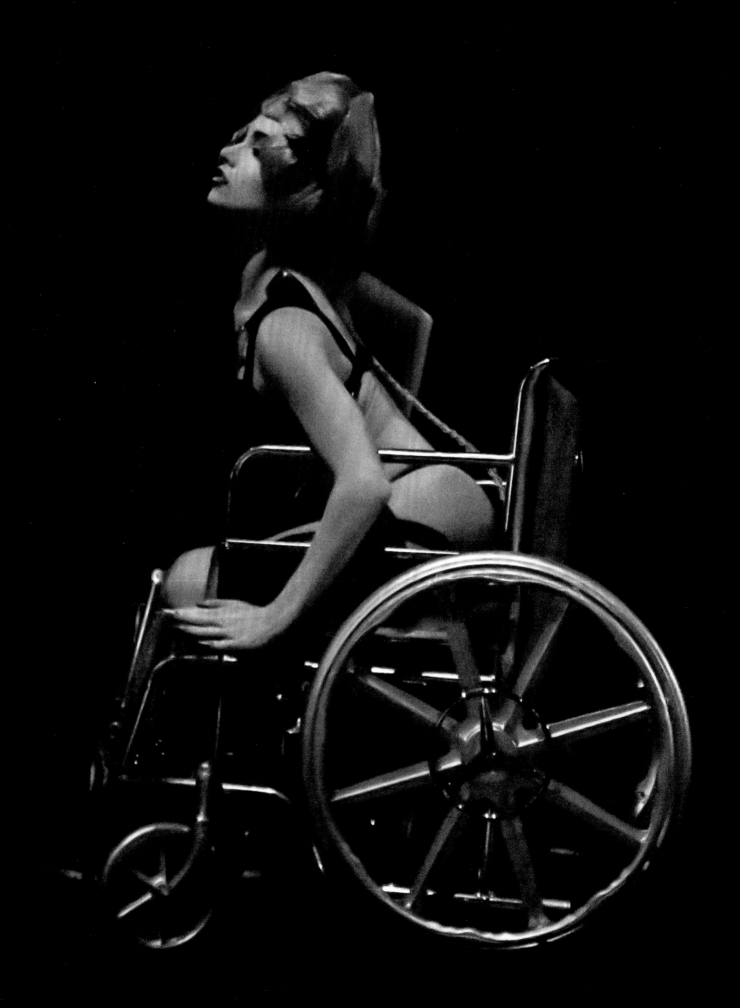

Charlie is extraordinary, unifying the craftsmanship of a hair stylist and wig-maker with the creativity of an avant-garde artist and fashion designer. It's wonderful to see our clients' amazement when we present his creations. He strives for perfection in everything he does, and he encourages stylists to enter new levels of creativity and craftsmanship. Charlie has a unique visual language, and that rare ability to create something totally new and different with every new collection, while maintaining his own distinctive style. This is what differentiates a truly great artist.

—Ingrid Batruel, CEO, Hairdreams

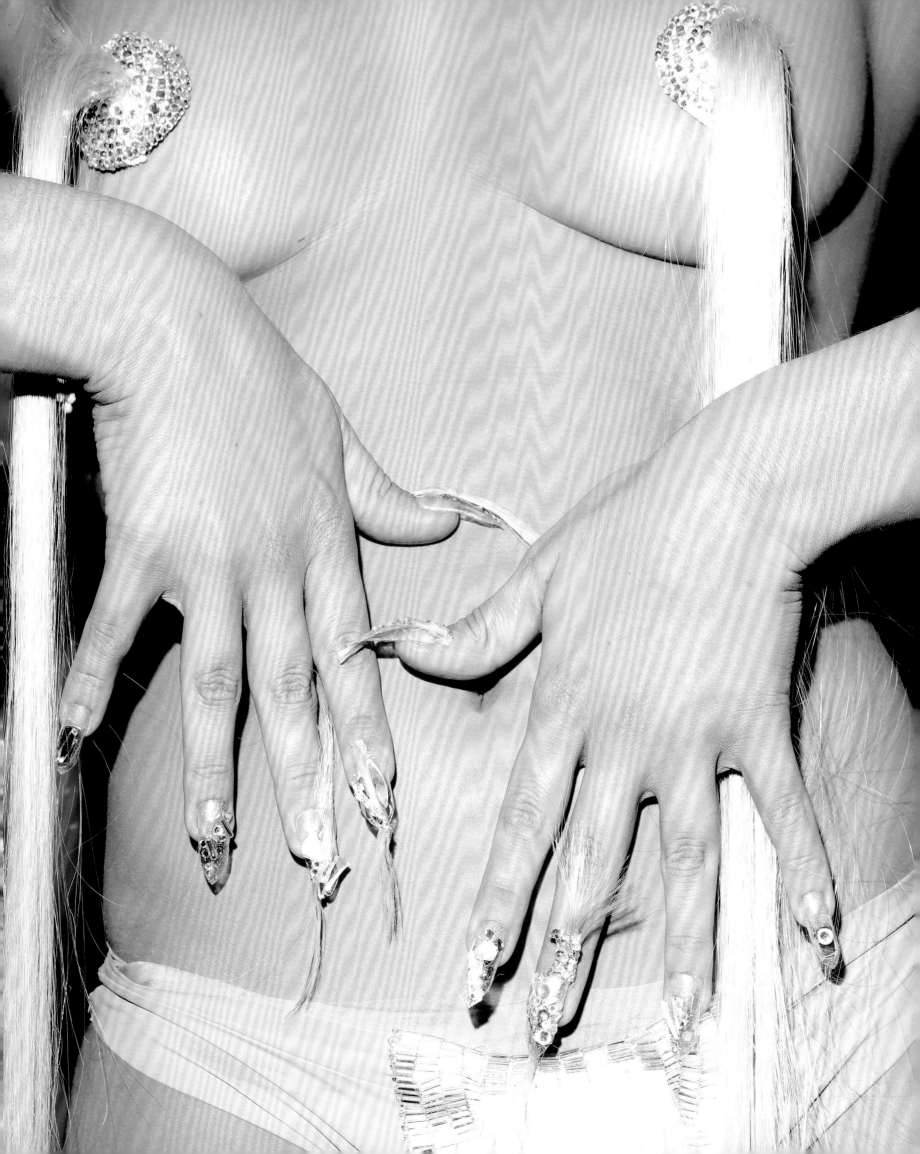

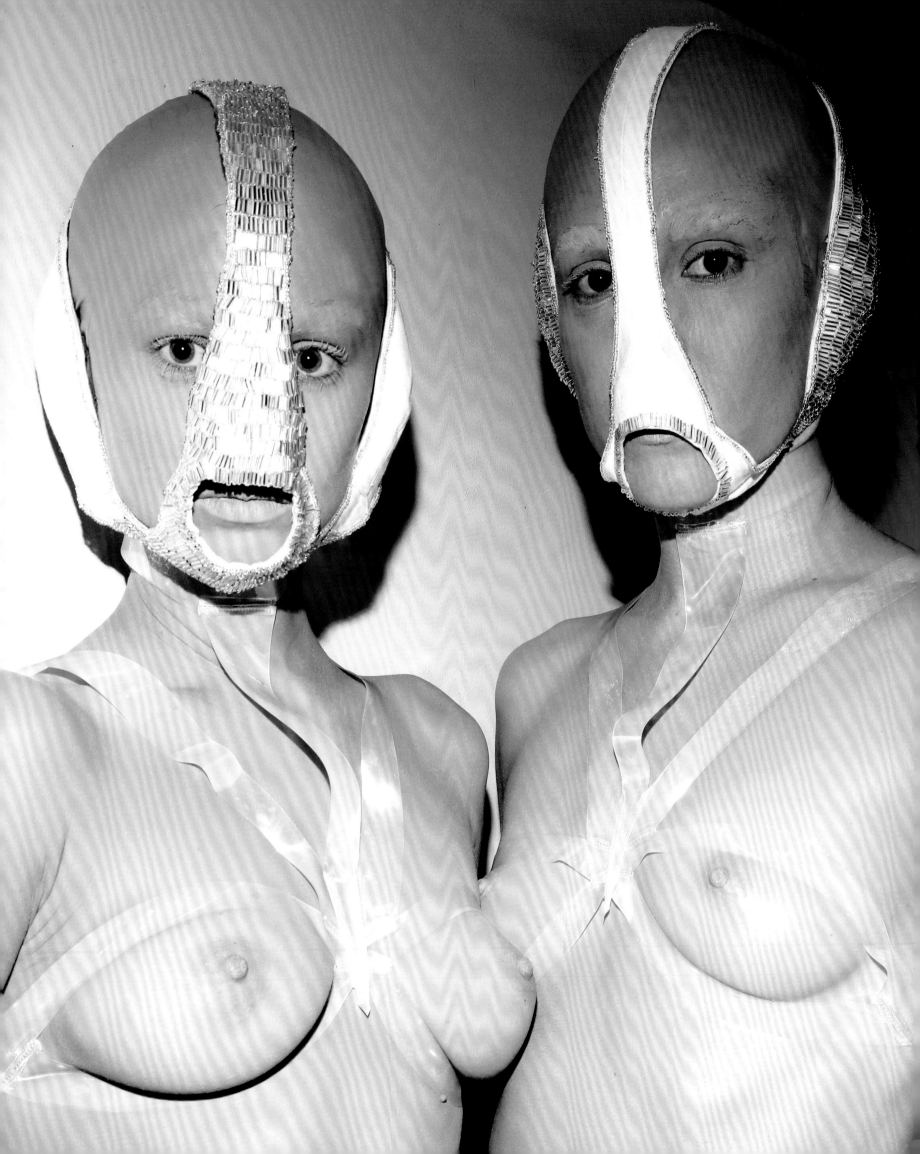

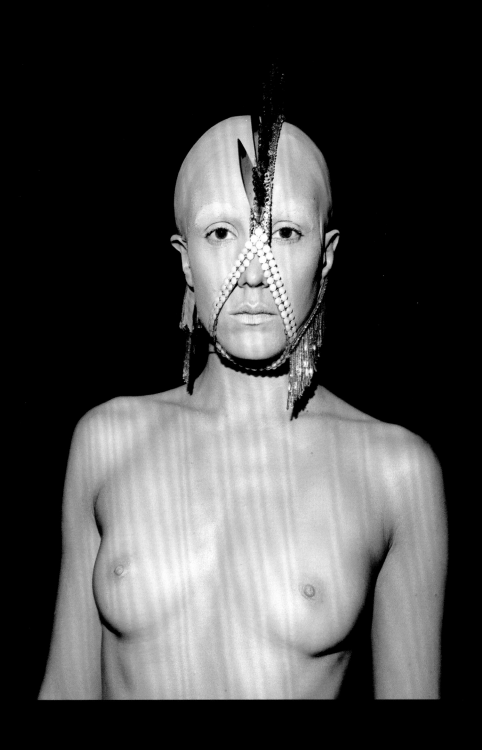

Credits

Special thanks to:

Thibault Pradet, Anna Trevelyan, Caroline Martial, Orion Bouvier, Coralie Ruiz, Liz Bisou, Stéphane Margolis, Shiori Takahashi, Thomas Petherick, Jamie Bull, MIMI, Peaches, Marina Gasolina … for inspiring my work so much.